Rough Guides

25 Ultimate experiences

New Zealand

Make the most of your time on Earth

25 YEARS 1982–2007

NEW YORK • LONDON • DELHI

Contents

Introduction

EXPERIENCES have always been at the heart of the Rough Guide concept. A group of us began writing the books **25 years ago** (hence this celebratory mini series) and wanted to share the kind of travels we had been doing ourselves. It seems bizarre to recall that in the early 1980s, travel was very much a minority pursuit. Sure, there was a lot of tourism around, and that was reflected in the guidebooks in print, which traipsed around the established sights with scarcely a backward look at the local population and their life. We wanted to change all that: to put a country or a city's popular culture centre stage, to highlight the clubs where you could hear local music, drink with people you hadn't come on holiday with, watch the local football, join in with the festivals. And of course we wanted to push travel a bit further, inspire readers with the confidence and knowledge to break away from established routes, to find pleasure and excitement in remote islands, or desert routes, or mountain treks, or in street culture.

Twenty-five years on, that thinking seems pretty obvious: we all want to experience something real about a destination, and to seek out travel's **ultimate experiences**. Which is exactly where these **25 books** come in. They are not in any sense a new series of guidebooks. We're happy with the series that we already have in print. Instead, the **25s** are a collection of ideas, enthusiasms and inspirations: a selection of the very best things to see or do – and not just before you die, but now. Each selection is gold dust. That's the brief to our writers: there is no room here for the average, no space fillers. Pick any one of our selections and you will enrich your travelling life.

But first of all, take the time to browse. Grab a half dozen of these books and let the ideas percolate … and then begin making your plans.

Mark Ellingham
Founder & Series Editor, Rough Guides

25 Ultimate experiences

New Zealand

Few spectacles can match the terrifying sight of the All Blacks performing a haka before a test match. You feel a chill down your spine fifty metres away in the stands; imagine how it must feel facing it as an opponent. The intimidating thigh-slapping, eye-bulging, tongue-poking chant traditionally used is the **Te Rauparaha haka**, and like all such **Maori posture dances** it is designed to display fitness, agility and ferocity. This version was reputedly composed early in the nineteenth century by the warrior Te Rauparaha, who was hiding from his enemies in the sweet potato pit of a friendly chief. Hearing noise above and then being blinded by the sun when the pit covering was removed he thought his days were numbered, but as his eyes became accustomed to the light he saw the hairy legs of his host and was so relieved he performed the haka on the spot. It goes:

01 Witnessing the power of the
All Blacks' haka

Ka Mate! Ka Mate! It is death! It is death!
Ka Ora! Ka Ora! It is life! It is life!
Tenei te ta ngata puhuru huru This is the hairy man
Nana nei i tiki mai whakawhiti te ra Who caused the sun to shine
A upane, ka upane! Step upwards! Another step upward!
A upane, ka upane! Step upwards! Another step upward!
Whiti te ra! Into the sun that shines!

Over the last decade or so, descendants of tribes once defeated by Te Rauparaha took umbrage at the widespread use of this haka at rugby matches and consequently a replacement, the **Kapa o Pango** (Team in Black) haka, was devised. Numerous Maori experts were consulted over what form the haka should take but controversy still surrounds the final throat-slitting gesture, which is supposed to symbolize the harnessing of vital energy. It remains to be seen whether *Kapa o Pango* will replace the traditional haka, be used on special occasions (as apparently planned), or fade from view. But whichever you manage to catch, both versions still illicit that same spine-tingling response.

need to know

The All Blacks (ⓦwww.allblacks.com) perform a haka before every test match. The best chance of catching a game in New Zealand is during the Tri-Nations series between New Zealand, Australia and South Africa. From early July to mid-September each year there are three home tests, typically in Auckland, Wellington and Christchurch. Tickets start at NZ$50.

9

02

Taking in the views on the

Alpine tundra, barren volcanic craters, steaming springs and iridescent lakes – the sheer diversity on the Tongariro Crossing makes it probably the best one-day tramp in the country. The wonderfully long views are unimpeded by the dense bush that crowds most New Zealand tracks, and from the highest point you can look out over almost half the North Island with the lonely peak of **Mount Taranaki** dominating the western horizon.

The hike crosses one corner of the Tongariro National Park – wild and bleak country, encompassing the icy tops of nearby **Mount Ruapehu**, which is, at 2797m, the North Island's highest mountain. Catch the Crossing on a fine day and it is a hike of pure exhilaration. The steep slog up to the South Crater sorts out the genuinely fit from the aspirational, then just as the trail levels out, **Mount Ngauruhoe** (2291m) invites the keen for a two-hour side-trip up Ngauruhoe's scoria slopes. The reward is a stupendous view down into the gently steaming crater, and a longer one of the rest of the Crossing. Getting back on track is a heart-pounding hell for leather scree run back down the mountain coving, in fifteen minutes what took you an hour and a half to ascend.

Tongariro Crossing

need to know

The 16km Tongariro Crossing involves around 750m of ascent and 1000m of descent and typically takes 6–8hr. A drop-off and pick-up bus deal from the town of National Park costs NZ$25. The climate between November and April makes these the most popular months, but at any time be sure to take food, water, strong shoes and warm, waterproof gear no matter how benign the weather appears.

The gaping gashes and sizzling fissures around **Red Crater** make it a lively spot to tuck into your sandwiches and ponder the explosive genesis of this whole region. From here it is mostly downhill past **Emerald Lake**, its opaque waters a dramatic contrast to the shimmering surface of **Blue Lake** just ahead. With the knowledge you've broken the back of the hike you can relax on the verandah of Ketetahi Hut gazing out over the tussock to glistening **Lake Taupo** in the distance. Rejuvenated, you pass the sulphurous **Ketetahi Hot Springs** on the final descent, down to the green forest and the welcome sight of your bus. Tired but elated you settle back in the seat dreaming of a good feed and the chance to relive the events of the day over a couple of beers.

It's **7.30am** and we're just a kilometre off the coast of Kaikoura. I can still see the wharf where we embarked, backed by **the snowcapped Seaward Kaikoura range**, and yet below us is 1000 metres of ocean. This is exactly the sort of territory that many whale species like to call home. Most places in the world, a whale-watching trip involves hours powering out to sea to the whales' migration route, but here the whales are virtually on the doorstep.

Sperm whales and **dusky dolphins** are year-round residents, while blue whales, pilot whales, and especially humpback whales all pass through. Regular visitors include southern right whales, so named because whalers found them to be the "right" whales to kill – they floated after being harpooned.

Weather permitting, trips run several times a day, and you're typically out among the leviathans within minutes. In fact, so confident are the tour operators that if you don't see a whale they'll refund 80% of your fee.

On the short journey out, big video screens have taken us into the virtual "World of the Whales" and their life in the depths of **the**

03
Watching *whales* in **Kaikoura**

Kaikoura Canyon and beyond, but we're here to see the real thing. Right on cue, someone spots **a plume of spray,** then a short dorsal fin. It is a humpback. The previously half-awake boat comes alive as everyone crowds the rails, camera in hand. Out of the corner of my eye I just catch a **thirty-tonne barnacled beast** surge out of the water, almost clearing the waves, with sheets of brine pouring off its sides. It crashes back with a surface rending splash. We're all thrilled at our good fortune and anticipating even greater displays when the whale decides it has had enough, and with a wave of its tail bids us adieu.

need to know

All boat-based whale-watching trips are run by the Maori-owned **Whale Watch Kaikoura** (☎03/319 5045, Ⓦwww.whalewatch.co.nz) who charge $130 for a two-and-a-half-hour tour. Sea conditions can be unpleasant and seasickness is not uncommon. The trips are very popular in summer; you'll need to book days (if not weeks) in advance.

Waitangi
the birth of a modern nation

On February 6 1840, representatives of the British Crown and several dozen northern Maori chiefs met in a marquee on the lawns in front of the Waitangi Treaty House to sign the **Treaty of Waitangi**. The Maori chiefs were rightly suspicious of British motivations and it remains debatable whether they knew they were signing away their sovereignty. It was a tense time, but sign they did, and the Treaty became not just New Zealand's founding document, but the cornerstone of the country's race relations to this day.

Arriving at the Treaty Grounds, you walk straight out onto that hallowed lawn with its views out over the Bay of Islands and its historic flagpole where Maori and British flags still fly. Inquisitive foreign visitors, and Kiwis in search of their heritage, gravitate towards **the 1834 Treaty House** itself, all neat white weatherboards and rooms containing material on the early colonial period.

When Maori arrived for the signing, most would have come by canoe but few would have been as big as *Ngatoki Matawhaorua*, now in residence down by the shore. The world's largest wooden war **canoe**, it stretches more than 35m from prow to gloriously carved sternpost and took over two years to carve from a pair of massive kauri tree trunks. Eighty warriors are needed to paddle it during its annual outing on the anniversary of the signing of the Treaty.

Lolling-tongue carved figures with iridescent seashell eyes greet you into *whare rununga*, or Maori meeting house, up beside the lawn – the only pan-tribal meeting house in the country.

For a deeper understanding of the *whare rununga*'s significance, return in the evening for the stirring **Night Show**. Through heartfelt dance, song and story-telling you'll get a primer in the richness of **Maori legend and history** and learn a good deal about modern Maori life and how the Treaty remains so essential to it.

need to know

During the day visit the Waitangi Visitor Centre and Treaty House (daily: Oct–March 9am–6pm; April–Sept 9am–5pm; NZ$12; @www.waitangi.net.nz). In the evening book ahead for the Night Show (Oct–March Mon, Wed, Thurs & Sat 8pm; NZ$50; ☎09/402 5990, @www.culturenorth.co.nz).

Taking a trip to hell on earth

You'll no doubt smell Rotorua before you even reach the city limits. It isn't known as the "Sulphur City" for nothing, and the bad-egg smell gets everywhere. Thankfully you get used to it after an hour or so...

The whole city sits on a thin crust of earth underlain by a seething cauldron of waters and superheated steam that seem desperate to escape. Walking around you'll see puffs of vapour rising out of people's backyards, and stormwater drains venting sulphurous jets. Crypts predominate in the cemeteries as graves can't be dug into the ground, and on the shores of Lake Rotorua gulls are relieved of the chore of sitting on their ground-built nests – the earth is warm enough to incubate without assistance.

need to know

There are a handful of major thermal areas around Rotorua. In town the best is Te Puia (daily: summer 8am–6pm; winter 8am–5pm; NZ$25; ⊛www.tepuia. co.nz) where you'll find the region's most reliable natural geyser, Pohutu. The most colourful pools combine with boiling mud and an artificially induced geyser around 30km south of Rotorua at Wai-o-Tapu (daily 8.30am–5pm; NZ$23; ⊛www. geyserland.co.nz).

"**I wish I had never seen the place, it reminds me too vividly of the fate theologians have promised me**".

George Bernard Shaw on visiting Rotorua's Hell's Gate thermal area in 1934.

Half a dozen spectacularly active areas are home to some dramatic geothermal wonders. Tourists have been flocking for over a century to see the Pohutu geyser, which regularly spouts to 20m; around the turn of the millennium it performed continuously for an unprecedented 329 days. It still spouts several times a day, a spectacular show that's heralded by the Prince of Wales Feathers geyser. Mineral deposits turn lakes wild shades of orange and green, and steam forces its way through the earth to form boiling mud pools patterned with myriad concentric circles.

Weary bones are also well-catered for in Rotorua – just about every motel and campground has a hot pool in which to soak. Make a point of seeking out genuine mineral ones filled by therapeutic geothermal waters, whether it be hydrothermal pampering in sophisticated resorts or back-to-basics natural pools out in the woods under the stars.

Cruising
Doubtful Sound

The smell of frying bacon wafting from the galley brings the boat awake. And what a place to wake up. Deathly still, there's mist clinging to the sides of the cliffs which hem in Doubtful Sound; the only movement comes from one lone soul who has borrowed one of the boat's kayaks and is out exploring the shoreline. Cruises on Milford Sound may be more famous, but Doubtful Sound, in the far southwest corner of the South Island, is equally spectacular and being off the main tourist route is a more intriguing place to visit. Just getting out here is half the fun. First a cruise across **Lake Manapouri**, a deep, glacier-hewn body of water that appears pristine, though it has been harnessed for power generation. You can even join a tour into the bowels of the earth to see the station, though it does seem at odds with the wilderness experience.

Finally, a bus ride carries you over the 670-metre high **Wilmot Pass** from where you get your first glimpse of Doubtful Sound, a hairline thread of water forcing its way 20km inland from the Tasman Sea. So narrow is the fiord that explorer **Captain Cook**, who named the place, didn't actually enter – he felt it was so confined that he was **doubtful** he would be able to get out again.

After a hearty breakfast we're underway again, gently exploring narrow channels where the thick forest creeps right down to the shoreline. Before long we're joined by a small group of **bottlenose dolphins**. It is hard to work out if these are our friends from yesterday come back to play, or others from the resident pod. Either way, they seem to be having a great time riding the bow wave on their side gazing up at us as we lean over the rail.

need to know

Trips start from either Te Anau or Manapouri in Fiordland National Park. **Real Journeys** (☎03/249 7416, ⓦwww.realjourneys.co.nz) run two excellent Doubtful Sound cruises, a one-day cruise (NZ$215) and an overnight cruise (from NZ$340) sleeping on the ship.

need to know

For a broad guide to locations visit ⓦwww.filmnz.com/middleearth/locations/index.html which gives a general idea of the regional spread. Numerous companies offer tours; for example, Hobbiton can be visited with **Rings Scenic Tours** (several daily; $50; ⓣ07/888 6838, ⓦwww.hobbitontours.com).

Discovering your own
Middle Earth

When Peter Jackson decided to film the *Lord of the Rings* trilogy entirely in New Zealand, he couldn't have known what a lasting impact it would have on his homeland. Even five years on, the country's scenery seems inextricably linked with that of Middle Earth. Familiar scenes abound. The black scoria cone of Ngauruhoe in Tongariro National Park is easily recognizable as the formidable Mount Doom. In the centre of the South Island, a smallish hill, Mount Sunday, rises from a wide valley – this is Edoras, the fortress city of the Rohan people. Getting there involves a gorgeous drive into the high country with the snowy Southern Alps as a backdrop. You can see the hill from the road, but it is worth trekking across the fields to reach the summit, where you can close your eyes and imagine the bleats of the sheep are the cries of hordes of invading orcs. There are more tangible reminders too. Although New Line Cinema went to great lengths to ensure that film sets were dismantled, Hobbiton managed to partially survive. You can now tour the partly restored set on a rolling green sheep farm (ahh, the Shire) a few kilometres outside the rural town of Matamata. Here, you can stand under the Party Tree where Bilbo Baggins held his eleventy-first birthday party with the village pond behind you and in front, a semicircle of hobbit holes cut into a shallow bowl in the undulating hills.

Plenty of tours can take you to movie locations, but the pleasure is not so much in visiting the scene as meeting people who were involved in some way. Chances are your driver was an orc, or your helicopter pilot flew influential crew members around, or you may even meet one of the horses used for the battle at Pelennor Field. Precioussssssss encounters indeed.

08

There's a knee-high yellow-eyed penguin preening itself less than five metres away from me, and fifteen metres beyond him, a sheep is grazing in lush meadows. It's an odd juxtaposition, probably one only to be found in New Zealand where, despite a lack of icebergs and tidewater glaciers, penguins abound. With two penguin species, a colony of seals and the world's only mainland Royal albatross colony, the Otago Peninsula is a fantastic place for a day's wildlife watching.

They're shy creatures these penguins, but here at Penguin Place they're barely aware of our presence. We're shoulder-deep in a dugout trench draped with camouflage netting, half a dozen of us huddled together in a strategically positioned hide overlooking fields, patches of wetland and a golden beach. As we walked over the hills to the trenches we saw a couple of penguins slowly waddling up the beach returning home from their day's fishing, but it's only in the hides that we get to see them up close as they do their ablutions. Most of the four or five birds out this afternoon are just grooming and watching the world go by, but the setting feels so intimate that I could watch for hours.

Dragging ourselves away, we head 10km up the road to Pilot's Beach where we wander among southern fur seals sprawled languidly along the shore. We'll be back here after dark to watch more penguins (little blues this time) toddle up the beach to their nesting holes in the bank.

On the hill above the beach, Taiaroa Head, we're guided into another hide, this one the converted remains of a WWII viewing tower. High on this grassy headland we can look out over a couple of dozen of Royal albatrosses – a truly majestic bird with up to a 3.5-metre wingspan. Quite a sight in full flight. It's mid-summer and the chicks are growing nicely, but are still vulnerable and spend most of their time tucked under a parent's wing. With binoculars you can see their fluffy heads poking out, desperate to learn more about the big world out there. They'll get their chance soon enough and spend their lives circling the globe before returning here every two years to breed.

need to know

The 35km Otago Peninsula starts in the suburbs of New Zealand's main southern city, Dunedin. It is an easy and scenic drive to all the spots mentioned including Penguin Place (℡03/478 0286, Ⓦwww.penguinplace.co.nz; NZ$33) and the Royal Albatross Centre (tours late Nov to mid-Sept daily; NZ$30; Ⓦwww.albatross.org.nz).

along the Otago Peninsula

Standing on a cold riverbank on a misty morning might not sound like much fun, especially when you know that soon you are going to get very wet. Such considerations evaporate when a chopper swoops around the side of a mountain and picks up your small team and its raft.

Seconds later you're in a plastic bubble skimming the tops of the ancient West Coast forests as you follow the river upstream. From above the river looks tame enough, but the reality is something else altogether. In no time you're in untouched wilderness, the fear building as the guides pump up the rafts and run you through the safety drill. And this is no litigation-conscious cover-your-back spiel; there's big water up ahead so guides and guests are mutually reliant for everyone's safety. You can expect around five hours on the water, often getting out to scout upcoming rapids, picking a line then paddling like hell to punch through a wave or avoid a hole. Some of the most thrilling and scenic whitewater trips in the world are offered here (many only explored in the last twenty years) – dramatically steep, they spill out of the alpine wilderness fed by the prodigious quantity of rain that guarantees solid flows. The steepness of the terrain means you're in Grade IV–V territory, so this isn't the right choice for novices. Companies in Rotorua and Queenstown run excellent low-cost trips for first-timers, but connoisseurs will delight in the challenges of West Coast rafting. It's truly heart-thumping stuff, making the wind-down time in a classic rural pub afterwards all the more enjoyable.

need to know

There are fabulous rafting rivers right down the West Coast of the South Island. Most require helicopter access so prices are fairly high, but the rewards easily justify them. Two of the best companies are **Ultimate Descents** (℡0800/748 377, ⓦwww.rivers.co.nz) in the north of the region, and Rivers Wild (℡0800/469 453, ⓦwww.riverswild.co.nz) in the south. Fly-in full-day trips start around NZ$350.

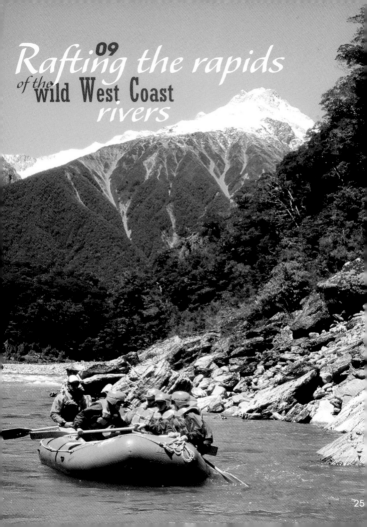

Rafting the rapids *of the* wild West Coast rivers

09

*W*hen Marlborough's *Cloudy Bay* sauvignon blanc hit the international wine shelves in the late 1980s its zingy fruitiness got jaded tongues wagging. All of a sudden New Zealand was on the world wine map, with the pushpin stuck firmly in the north of the South Island. Half a dozen regions now boast significant wine trails, but all roads lead back to Marlborough, still the country's largest grape growing area, protected by the sheltering hills of the Richmond Range, and blessed with more than 2400 hours of sunshine a year.

Cellar doors around the region are gradually becoming more sophisticated, with their own restaurants and specialist food stores, but the emphasis is still mainly on the wine itself. And tasting it. To squeeze the very best from the area start by visiting *Montana Brancott*, the biggest and most established operation hereabouts. Take their winery tour to get a feel for how wine is made nowadays, then stick around for a brief lesson on wine appreciation. Even those familiar with the techniques will learn something of the qualities Marlborough winemakers are trying to achieve.

Next visit *Cloudy Bay*. Of course you'll want to try the famous sav, still drinking well today and available for tasting. Somehow it always seems that little bit fresher and fruitier when sampled at source out of a decent tasting glass.

Come lunchtime, head for *Highfield Estate* with its distinctive Tuscan-style tower and dine in the sun overlooking the vines. A plate of pan-seared monkfish is just the thing to wash down with their zesty sauvignon blanc.

need to know

Visitor centres and most wineries stock a free map to the region's wineries which lists current opening hours (generally daily 10am–4pm or later). **Marlborough Tours** (℡03/573 7877, Ⓦwww.marlboroughtours.co.nz) offers a full-day minibus wine tour for NZ$60, or try a self-guided bicycle tour with **Wine Tours by Bike** (℡03/577 6954, Ⓦwww.winetoursbybike.co.nz), who charge NZ$55 for a full day's bike rental.

11

Exploring Waitomo's eerie

underground world

need to know

Most people take a walking tour through Waitomo Glowworm Caves (daily 9am–5pm; NZ$30). The Legendary Black Water Rafting Co. offer the Black Labyrinth (NZ$90), and the Black Abyss (NZ$150) which adds abseiling. The most adventurous tours are with Absolute Adventure NZ$175 who don't offer tubing or long abseils but give an authentic caving experience. Set aside a full day.

*W*aitomo, a tiny town in rolling sheep country, sits on a veritable Swiss cheese of limestone, with deep sinkholes, beautifully sculpted tunnels and wild organ pipes of stalactites all lit up by ghostly constellations of glowworms.

Traditionally the way to see all this is on a gentle stroll through some of the shallower caverns where the Victorian explorers named the flowstone formations after animals, mythical creatures and household items. Coloured lights pick out the salient features before you take an other-worldly ride in a dinghy across an underground lake; the green pinpricks of light above your head resembling the heavens of some parallel universe.

Ever the adventure pioneers, New Zealand has also created another method of exploring the caves – blackwater rafting. Decked out in wetsuit, helmet and miner's lamp you head underground with a truck inner tube, then sit in it and float through the gloom. The few rapids are gentle and safe but the blackness gives that extra frisson of uncertainty.

Assorted trips up the ante with hundred-metre-long abseils, waterfall jumping and even a little subterranean rock climbing. Or you could try a straightforward traditional caving trip. With small groups there's a genuine feeling of exploration as you negotiate tight squeezes, find your way into pristine rooms full of gossamer straws and maybe even fully submerge through sumps to access yet deeper recesses.

Ever since speed skiers and general daredevils AJ Hackett and Henry van Asch invented commercial bungy jumping, New Zealand has been its home, and Queenstown its capital.

So if you're going to bungy what better place than here? And if it's the classic experience you're after then the original Kawarau Suspension Bridge is your spot. At 43m it's only a modest jump by modern standards, but you're guaranteed an audience to will you on and then celebrate your achievement.

And the river is deep enough to allow a dunking – hands, head, full body, whatever you want, just ask. The operators usually get it spot on.

Diving off tall towers with vines tied around your ankles has been a male rite of passage in Vanuatu for centuries, but modern bungy started with the nutty antics of the Oxford University Dangerous Sports Club in the 1970s. The next leap forward was AJ Hackett's bungy off the Eiffel Tower in 1987. He was promptly arrested but soon started commercial operations in Queenstown.

So are you going solo or double? Dunking or not? Shirt on or shirt off? Decisions made, you stroll out onto the bridge (looking oh so casual) while pumping rock or hip hop starts building the adrenaline. Wrapping a towel around your ankles for protection, they'll attach the cord while feeding you some jocular spiel about the bungy breaking (it won't) or not being attached properly (it will be). You'll then be chivvied into producing a cheesy (or wan) grin for the camera before shuffling out onto the precipice for the countdown.

Three. Two. One. Bungy!

12

Taking the plunge with AJ Hackett

need to know

AJ Hackett Bungy (☎0800/286 495, 🅦www .ajhackett.com) regularly operate three bungy sites around Queenstown. A jump at the original 43m Kawarau site costs NZ$140; you'll pay NZ$140 to bungy at the 47m Urban Ledge site on a hill above Queenstown; and need to stump up NZ$199 for the massive 134m Nevis Bungy. All jumps include a bragging rights T-shirt.

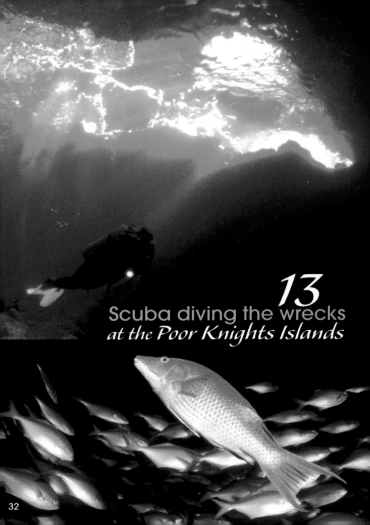

13
Scuba diving the wrecks
at the Poor Knights Islands

*J*acques Cousteau championed the Poor Knights Islands as one of the top ten dive sites in the world, fairly weighty praise from a man with his extensive marine knowledge. And with their warm currents, visibility regularly around 30m and a host of undersea attractions his judgement is understandable. Dive boats spread themselves over 50 recognized dive sites, which jointly cover New Zealand's most *diverse range of sea life* including subtropical species, such as Lord Howe coralfish and toadstool grouper, found nowhere else around the coast.

Near-vertical rock faces drop 100m through a *labyrinth of caves*, fissures and rock arches teeming with rainbow-coloured fish, crabs, soft corals, kelp forests and shellfish. Blue, humpback, sei and minke whales also drop in from time to time, and dolphins are not uncommon.

A typical day might include an hour-long cruise out to the islands followed by a drift dive through a sandy-bottomed cave populated by stingrays and lit by *shafts of sunlight*. After lunch on board and perhaps some time paddling one of the boat's kayaks you'll head around the coast to a second dive spot, maybe working your way along a *technicolour wall of soft corals* and a few nudibranchs.

As if that weren't enough, the waters north and south of the reserve are home to two *navy wrecks*, both deliberately scuttled. The survey ship HMNZS Tui was sunk in 1999 to form an artificial reef, and it was so popular with divers and marine life that the obsolete frigate Waikato followed two years later. These form part of a Northland wreck trail which includes the remains of the Greenpeace flagship Rainbow Warrior, bombed by French government agents in 1985 just before it set out to campaign against French nuclear testing in the Pacific.

need to know

The Poor Knights Islands are a marine reserve 25km off the east coast of Northland, towards the northern tip of New Zealand. **Dive! Tutukaka** (℗0800/288 882, ⓦwww. diving.co.nz) run numerous trips from the small port of Tutukaka. A two-tank full-day dive trip with all gear to either the Poor Knights or the wrecks goes for NZ$200.

14
TUCKING INTO A
hangi

Asuitably reverential silence descends, broken only by munching and appreciative murmurs from the assembled masses – the hangi has finally been served. This traditional Maori fare, similar to the luau prepared by the Maori people's Polynesian kin in Hawaii, is essentially a feast cooked in an earth oven for several hours. It can't be found on restaurant menus – but then again a hangi is not just a meal, it's an event.

need to know

The ideal way to experience a hangi (pronounced nasally as "hungi") is as a guest at a private gathering of extended families. Most people don't have this option, however, so the alternative is to join one of the commercial affairs. Although you'll be a paying customer rather than a guest, the hangi will be no less authentic. Rotorua in the North Island has many options, usually as part of an evening concert-and-hangi combo for which you'll pay around NZ$80. Mitai (℡07/343 9132, 🌐www.mitai.co.nz) is particularly good.

To begin, the men light a fire, and once it has burned down, specially selected river stones that don't splinter are placed in the embers. While these are heating, a large pit is dug, perhaps two metres square and a metre and a half deep. Meanwhile the women are busy preparing lamb, pork, chicken, fish, shellfish and vegetables (particularly kumara, the New Zealand sweet potato). Traditionally these would be wrapped in leaves then arranged in baskets made of flax; these days baking foil and steel mesh are more common.

When everything is ready (the prep can take up to three hours), the hot stones are placed in the pit and covered with wet sacking. Then come the baskets of food followed by a covering of earth which serves to seal in the steam and the flavours. There's a palpable sense of communal anticipation as hosts and guests mill around chatting and drinking, waiting for the unearthing. A couple of hours later, the baskets are disinterred, revealing fall-off-the-bone steam-smoked meat and fabulously tender vegetables with a faintly earthy flavour. A taste, and an occasion, not easily forgotten.

Heli-hiking on **Franz Josef glacier**

After the chopper banks away and the thwump-thwump-thwump of the rotors has receded down the glacier I'm left standing in a beautiful white silence. With half a dozen others and a guide I've got the next couple of hours to explore the upper reaches of Franz Josef glacier, one of a pair of blinding rivers of ice that cascade almost to sea level on the western side of the South Island's Southern Alps. In Maori legend these are *Ka Riomata o Hinehukatere* – "The Tears of the Avalanche Girl". The story goes that the beautiful Hinehukatere so loved the mountains that she encouraged her lover, Tawe, to climb alongside her. He fell to his death and Hinehukatere cried so copiously that her tears formed the glaciers.

The guide checks everyone has put on their crampons correctly and, stout stick in hand, we set off slowly working our way through a labyrinth of seracs (ice towers) and crevasses. It is a bit of a shock to the system and initially nerve-wracking as I gaze down into the blue depths of the glacier

with teetering blocks of ice looming above. But the guide seems to know what she's doing, continually assessing the changes on this fast-moving glacier. Most of the hikers have never been anywhere like this before so she charts a course that is safe but keeps us on our toes. Just as I am beginning to feel comfortable she ratchets up the exposure along a knife-edge ridge, just to make sure we're keeping our wits about us.

need to know

For reliable service at the best prices try **The Guiding Company** (☎0800/800 102, ⓦwww. nzguides.com) who charge NZ$320. They also have a number of cheaper trips involving hiking on the lower reaches of the glacier, NZ$80 for a half-day and NZ$135 for the superior full-day trip, which gets you a decent way up onto the glacier.

The ridge leads to a series of ice caves, features you couldn't hope to experience on hikes lower down the glacier. Deep blue and gently sculpted, they're wonderfully enticing and the guide leads us through. A little scrambling, crouching and sliding against the slippery walls and we've made it. Feeling confident, a couple of us are keen for something more challenging and we're shown a narrow hole that looks way too small to get past. Stripping off as much clothing as the temperature will allow we manage to worm our way into a glorious glowing grotto where we sit for a few minutes before struggling elated (and cold) back to the surface.

All too soon we hear the beat of the helicopter coming to whisk us back to town. Still, that means a steaming cup of hot chocolate is only fifteen minutes away – much needed after these dazzling few hours on the ice.

16
Spotting kiwi
on Stewart Island

There's nothing quite like the kiwi, an odd, flightless, nocturnal bird that has a curious way of endearing everyone to its enigmatic ways. Stout, muscular and shy, they spend much of the night using the nostrils at the end of their long bill to detect earthworms and beetles. Probing the ground, they make full use of their sense of smell, a great rarity in the bird world.

Once numerous all over the country, New Zealand's national symbol is now endangered, having fallen prey to introduced predators – primarily stoats. Sighting them in the wild is an uplifting, and rare, experience.

Of the half a dozen or so places in New Zealand where kiwi encounters are most common, one of the best is at Mason Bay on Stewart Island, 24km south of the South Island. The uninhabited western side is a wild and isolated place, backed by a golden beach and battered by southerly winds. It has long been abandoned by the early European farmers who tried to make a living here, and that's the way the kiwi seem to like it.

Since these little guys only venture out after dark you'll have to stay overnight. On a typical summer evening there'll be around twenty people in the bay's one fairly primitive hut, cooking over camping stoves and sharing the day's tales. Around an hour after dark (approaching midnight), everyone troops out with headtorches and flashlights, the light softened by a red-coloured gel, handed out by the hut warden. Kiwi are shy, so everyone creeps quietly along paths hoping for a sighting in the long grass. At first you just hear the birds calling to each other, perhaps warning their mates of the presence of humans. With luck they'll show themselves, suddenly emerging from the side of the grassy track and running along it in their waddling fashion before ducking for cover again. If you're very patient and still, you might even have one probing the ground around your feet: a rare treat indeed.

After an hour or so everyone files back to their bunks, elated at having encountered these curious birds at close quarters.

need to know Small planes and a ferry connect the South Island with Stewart Island's only town, Oban. From there you can walk to Mason Bay (2 days), take a water taxi most of the way then walk the last 4hr (NZ$50 each way) or fly, landing on the beach. Perhaps the best bet is the flight and water taxi combo (NZ$155). Everyone stays communally at the Department of Conservation hut (NZ$5) – buy a hut ticket from the DOC office in Oban, Stewart Island's only town.

Relaxing at the seaside in Art Deco Napier

With enough to keep you entertained but not so much to wear you out, Napier, a small provincial city on the east coast of the North Island, is perfect for a few days of leisure.

Its chief attraction is its small-scale Art Deco architecture, the result of a uniform building program after the place was devastated by an earthquake in 1931. Hundreds of lives were lost as fires swept through the rubble of the town. But Napier rose from the ashes adopting the precepts of the Art Deco movement prevalent at the time, albeit in a more subdued style informed by the Great Depression still biting hard. Today you'll see an unusually harmonious downtown of asymmetric buildings popping with chevrons, ziggurats, fountains (a symbol of renewal) and lightning flashes. While predominantly Art Deco, Napier's buildings were also given elements of earlier styles and the city ended up with a palimpsest of early-twentieth-century design, combining aspects of the Arts and Crafts movement, the Californian Spanish Mission style, Egyptian and Mayan motifs, the stylized floral designs of Art Nouveau, the blockish forms associated with Charles Rennie Mackintosh, and even Maori imagery. A case in point is the **ASB Bank**, its exterior adorned with fern shoots and a mask form from the head of a *taiaha* (a long fighting club), while its interior has a fine Maori rafter design.

The up-and-coming harbour area of **Ahuriri** has perhaps Napier's finest example, the **National Tobacco Company Building**, which exhibits a decorative richness seldom seen on industrial buildings. The facade merges Deco asymmetry and the classic juxtaposition of cubic shapes and arches with the softening Art Nouveau motifs of roses and raupo (a kind of Kiwi bulrush).

But Napier's not just pretty architecture, it's also an idyllic seaside setting. Take a stroll along the beachside Marine Parade, an antipodean imprint of a classic British seafront with an aquarium, a sunken flower garden and an excellent modernized Lido-style pool complex, and don't miss the curvaceous bronze statue of *Pania of the Reef*, a legendary Maori sea-maiden whose body now forms the rocky shoals just offshore.

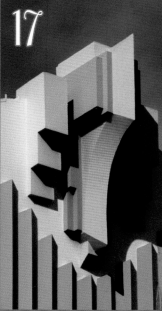

need to know

The Art Deco Shop, 163 Tennyson St (daily 9am–5pm), offers a free 20min Deco video and sells a map for a self-guided Art Deco Walk (NZ$4). Dedicated Deco buffs meet here for the guided walking tours (1–2 daily; NZ$10–15) lasting one to two hours.

18 Tramping the Milford track

You're going to get wet on this tramp. In fact it would be disappointing if you didn't. When the heavens open it seems like the hills are leaking; every cliff-face springs a waterfall and the rivers quickly become raging torrents.

The Milford Track lies in **Fiordland National Park**, most of which gets at least five metres of rain a year, making it one of the wettest places in the world. But unless you are really unlucky it won't rain the whole time. Blue skies reveal a wonderment of magical scenery best seen from **Mackinnon Pass**, the highest point of the tramp, at 1073m. Deep glaciated valleys drop steeply away on both sides while weather-worn mountains rear up all around. It is a great place to eat your lunch, always keeping a wary eye out for kea, New Zealand's cheeky alpine parrot, who will be off with your sandwiches given even a quarter of a chance.

From here you can see most of the Milford Track route. Behind you is the valley of the **Clinton River**, along which you've just spent a day and a half tramping, after being

dropped off by a small launch on the shores of Lake Te Anau. Ahead is the **Arthur River**, where the rain puts on its best display with two spectacular waterfalls. The story goes that when blazing the route in 1880, explorers Donald Sutherland and John Mackay came upon one magnificent fall, and tossed a coin to decide who would name it on the understanding that the loser would name the next one. Mackay won the toss but rued his good fortune when, days later, they stumbled across the much more famous and lofty **Sutherland Falls**, at 580m the tallest in New Zealand.

need to know

From late October to late April, independent walkers aiming to complete a Te Anau-based loop must book (Ⓦwww.doc.govt. nz) and pay NZ$120 for three nights hut accommodation, also reckoning on around NZ$140 for boat and bus transport. Everyone walks in the same direction and stays at the huts in sequence with no backtracking or extra nights. There is no camping.

A guided walk (Ⓣ03/441 1138, Ⓦwww.ultimatehikes.co.nz) requires much less effort, offers greater comforts, and costs around NZ$1750.

Setting sail among the blissful
Bay of Islands

We've lowered the sails, dropped anchor beside a gorgeous crescent of golden beach, and it's time for a swim before lunch. **The waters are warm and clear** in Northland's Bay of Islands, perfect territory for some gentle **cruising** and a touch of **snorkelling**. Our anchorage is just off Roberton Island where an isthmus is almost severed by a pair of perfectly circular blue lagoons. Mask on, I'm off to find the undersea nature trail where points of interest have been marked on little stainless steel plaques. It is fun but atypical of a region where **nature in its rawest form** is more usual.

After a lunch of **fresh barbecued fish** on deck we move slowly on past **Black Rocks**, bare islets formed from columnar jointed basalt – these rise only 10m out of the water but plummet a sheer 30m beneath, allowing us to inspect them at close quarters. We're aboard the R Tucker Thompson, a modern replica of a gaff rigged, square topsail schooner built in Northland in the style of a North American Halibut schooner. A majestic sight from afar, with the sails pushing out towards the open ocean, its even better aboard. You can help set the sails, ride the bowsprit, **climb the rigging** or just **laze on deck** playing the ship's guitar.

Occasionally dolphins will come and ride the boat's bow wave, but to really get close and personal with these fascinating mammals you need to get out on Carino, a smaller, modern yacht licensed for **dolphin swimming**. If a pod is spotted nearby, a handful of swimmers are immediately in the water splashing about and humming, trying to attract the dolphins' interest. Ever curious, dolphins seem to love the attention and are soon darting around, close but somehow always just out of reach.

need to know

A 6hr day aboard the **R. Tucker Thompson** (℡0800/882 537, Ⓦwww.tucker.co.nz) costs NZ$110. **Carino** (℡09/402 8040, Ⓦwww.sailingdolphins.co.nz) goes out for NZ$75, plus NZ$5 for a barbecue lunch.

TE PAPA
OUR PLACE
™

Getting hands on at Wellington's
Te Papa

Since 1998, Wellington's magnificent waterfront has been dominated by the Museum of New Zealand, which is always known by its shortened Maori name of Te Papa, loosely translated as "Our Place".

A far cry from the stuffy glass cases of the old museum it replaced, it exudes a radical modern approach not just in the design of the building itself but in the way the exhibits invite interaction and involvement.

Like any good museum it works on several levels and yet, despite its size, it never feels overwhelming. You can easily waltz through in a couple of hours and get a pretty comprehensive overview of what makes New Zealand tick. To make the most of your visit, linger over the

20

superb Maori section with its robustly carved war canoe, traditional houses, collections of fearsome war clubs and intricately worked jade jewellery. Displays showcase how people have migrated to New Zealand, first using the stars to navigate the Pacific in double-hulled canoes, later in sailing ships, and through to recent patterns of immigration from east Asia. And you shouldn't miss the marae, a Maori meeting place that is dramatically different from the red, black and white wood carvings you'll see elsewhere. Here semi-mythological figures are fashioned from warped plywood and shaded in an eye-catching array of pastel tones.

With more time on your hands, there's plenty to keep you occupied – drawers reveal smaller artefacts, a gallery showcases the best in Kiwi painting and sculpture, and "sound posts" encourage you to tune into wide-ranging views about the ongoing debate on New Zealand's founding document, the Treaty of Waitangi.

It's a great place for kids too, with all kinds of interactive, hands-on displays, the chance to experience what it felt like to be in New Zealand's most powerful earthquake and even some high-tech rides.

Almost a decade after its opening, over a million people pass through its doors every year. Not bad for a country with a population of three million. It must be doing something right.

need to know

Te Papa (Ⓦwww.tepapa.govt.nz) is open daily 10am–6pm and stays open until 9pm on Thursday. Entry is free, though there is a fee for the changing roster of special exhibits.

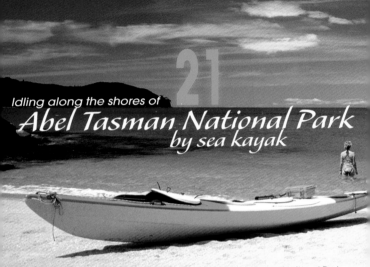

Idling along the shores of
Abel Tasman National Park
by sea kayak

Some people hike along the coast of Abel Tasman National Park, others cruise through its glassy waters, but by far the best way to explore New Zealand's smallest and most intimate national park is by sea kayak. The sheltering arm of Farewell Spit ensures the waters are seldom rough, so even completely inexperienced paddlers can head out for several days in relative safety.

Above all, this type of trip is about enjoying yourself at a relaxed tempo. And not only can you take to the shore at a pace that exactly suits you, but also the kayak can carry the load of all the wine, beer and tasty delicacies you'll want to bring along. A wide choice of golden beaches with designated camping spots are at your disposal to stop and indulge in your goodies, spend the afternoon lazing on the sand, explore rock pools or take a dip. Pack a mask and snorkel so you can watch the shoals of fish weaving among the rocks and kelp beds.

It is tempting to stay put for one more lazy day, but there are still more winding estuaries to paddle. You can also explore vestiges of human occupation that date back 150 years, before this area was set aside as protected land. The stub of a wharf marks the spot where granite was quarried and you can search out the quarry and grub surrounds looking for the foundations of quarrymen's huts.

Most people rent kayaks in Marahau or one of the other small towns at the southern end of the park. Expect to pay NZ$180 to rent a single kayak for four days, enough to see most of the coast. If you get tired you can flag down a water taxi and zip back to base in a few minutes. Campgrounds cost NZ$10, while a bunk in a simple hut costs NZ$25. Lodges include **Awaroa Lodge** (Ⓦwww.awaroalodge.co.nz) which charges NZ$300 a room.

One essential stop is the Tonga Island Marine Reserve, where the rocks come slathered with seals. These playful creatures have been known to come up to swimmers and cavort for a while before deciding there is something more entertaining happening elsewhere.

When you crave something a little more sophisticated than dinner cooked over a camp stove, wend your way up the delightful estuary of the Awaroa River, where a few lodges inhabit patches of private land. Stop in for a sandwich and an espresso or a beer on the deck; if you're feeling flush and hankering for white linen you can stay the night. A perfect finale to a glorious few days of relaxation.

Filling up in Auckland

Balinese black sticky rice with tropical fruit, coconut cream and palm sugar. Cured salmon bagel with Japanese pickles and wasabi cream cheese. Lemon and dill potato hash cakes with asparagus, poached eggs and smoked paprika hollandaise. Is your mouth watering yet? How about banana and chocolate loaf with berry preserve and yoghurt or maybe brioche french toast with blueberries and coffee mascarpone?

These aren't the offerings of a swanky New York hotel breakfast menu but pickings from a handful of **Auckland's cafés**. Invariably, you'll also be treated to superb coffee and the service will be **casual and friendly**, with a minimum of ceremony. Is it any wonder then that Aucklanders' favourite thing to do is to head out on the weekend to the dozens of suburban eateries dishing up such sumptuous selections? Although cafés are a particular Auckland speciality, at the ready for a laid-back meal or a simple coffee and slice of homemade carrot cake, often until late evening, Auckland's **dynamic food scene** is such that you'll be spoilt for choice if you're after a more formal meal too.

Globe-trotting chefs return to NZ's shores brimming with **innovative Pacific-Rim versions of more traditional dishes**. And what's more they have the very best of nature's offerings to play with. This clean, green land produces not only the top-notch **lamb** the country is so famous for but just about every **fruit** and vegetable that will withstand the Kiwi climate. Ingredients once alien in these parts are now cultivated; **groves of olive trees** produce oil that rivals any imported varieties, oak trees have been planted to establish a **truffle industry**, and **cheese-makers** tired of replicating traditional European varieties now create their own concoctions, often with great aplomb. Let's not forget either, that with harbours on both the Pacific and Tasman coasts, **Auckland is particularly blessed with its seafood**. When it's all expertly put together and served with a smile, you'd be hard-pressed to dine out better anywhere in the world. Who's hungry?

need to know

Benediction, 30 St Benedicts St, Newton (☏09/309 5001); **Atlas**, 285 Ponsonby Rd, (☏09/360 1295); and **Occam**, 135 Williamson Ave, Grey Lynn (☏09/378 0604), are just three Auckland cafés where your tastebuds will be tickled, though almost anywhere on Ponsonby Road is a winner. For more formal evening dining try **The Grove**, St Patrick's Square (☏09/368 4129), or **La Zeppa**, 33 Drake St (☏09/379 8167), for an Auckland spin on tapas.

23 Queenstown's winter wonderland

Queenstown is definitely the place to be in winter. For a start it has some of the best skiing and boarding in New Zealand with two excellent fields right on its doorstep. It is also extremely picturesque, snuggled alongside the waters of Lake Wakatipu and **hemmed in by snowcapped mountains**, not least the aptly named Remarkables. So far so standard for ski resorts, but in Queenstown you can also partake in "summer" activities at the same time. Suitably wetsuited, **whitewater rafters** run the Shotover and Kawarau rivers, and the **bungy site** above the town comes alive most nights in winter for floodlit leaps.

Always popular with Kiwis, Queenstown also draws Australians and addicts from the northern hemisphere who can't get enough action in their own ski season. As for the slopes, they're bald. None of your slaloming through trees here: this is all open vistas (and high winds when it blows). With **more than 400 vertical metres of skiing** and the longest pedigree of any Kiwi skifield, Coronet Peak is probably the more popular of the two fields. The Remarkables maxes out at 500 vertical metres and has its adherents, as much for the **fine off-piste terrain** as for the forgiving groomed slopes.

By world standards, Kiwi fields are quite primitive. Sure they have fast quad chairlifts and the like, but on-site facilities are limited to a few restaurants and bars. But that means you get to spend more time back in Queenstown where the **après ski** is second to none. The restaurants are easily the match

of those in Auckland and Wellington and the nightlife ranges from lively dance clubs to chic joints where you need to know the doorman to get in.

The season typically runs from early June into October, but the time to come is the last week of June for the **Queenstown Winter Festival** – a real riot with heaps of activities, crazy stunts and, of course, plenty of carousing.

need to know

The two major skifields are both run by NZSki.com (☎03/442 4640). A day lift pass at Coronet Peak costs NZ$84 while at The Remarkables it is NZ$79. Slightly cheaper multiday passes and season passes give access to both fields. Shuttle buses run continuously from Queenstown to both fields. For more on the festival check out Ⓦwww.winterfestival.co.nz.

Lazing about at Hot Water Beach

ike beaches? Like soaking in hot springs? Combine the two at Hot Water Beach where the receding tide reveals bath temperature water welling up through the sands. It's a beautiful thing to experience, but timing is crucial. Arrive at full tide and there'll be hardly anyone around. Sure the beach is a gorgeous strand of golden sand, but this part of New Zealand doesn't lack for gorgeous beaches.

Sometime around mid-tide you can wander down to the water edge and wriggle your toes down to feel the primal warmth below. An hour or so later families, backpackers and just about anyone with a sybaritic bent will be stopping in at the local shop renting a shovel and joining the throng on the beach. There's quite a communal spirit as people dig into the sand to create a network of shallow pools bolstered by sand embankments. You might have to pick your spot to find the optimum temperature, and at least part of the time you're likely to have surges of cool sea water easing the warmth. Hang around too long and the incoming tide gradually eats away at your defences – it's a good idea to enlist some dam-building kids to stem the tide for as long as possible if you can.

When you feel like you've cooked enough, you can always take a refreshing plunge in the sea. Be careful though, as this isn't the safest beach. Pacific breakers create powerful undertows and even strong swimmers should bathe with caution. With two low tides a day, chances are one will be at a convenient time.

Perhaps the best are those that fall in the evening close to full moon: take down a bottle of wine and settle in to gaze up at the stars.

need to know

The small settlement of Hot Water Beach is on the east coast of the North Island's Coromandel Peninsula, around 35km southeast of Whitianga. The best time is around an hour and a half either side of low tide. Local visitor centres all have tide tables. The local café/shop will rent you a spade for NZ$4.

New Zealand's South Island is vertically split by the Southern Alps, a snow-capped spine of 3000-metre-high mountains. Only three road passes breach this barrier, and just one rail line – the TranzAlpine. Slicing 225km across the South Island from Christchurch, the island's biggest city, to the small West Coast town of Greymouth, this unassuming train offers one of the most scenic train journeys in the world.

Don't come looking for a luxury experience. This certainly isn't the Orient Express, but any shortcomings of the train itself will fade into the background when you take a look out of the window – the scenery is mind-bogglingly spectacular, especially in winter, when it's at its most dramatic with the landscape cloaked in snow.

As the train eases out of Christchurch, urban back gardens give way to the open vistas of the Canterbury Plains, a swathe of bucolic sheep country carved into large paddocks. After an hour the rail line cuts away from the main highway and charts its own course past the dry grasslands of the Torlesse Range, gradually climbing all the while.

The west of the South Island gets huge amounts of rain, the east very little. Here you're in a transition zone, and with every kilometre you'll notice the character of the vegetation change. Subalpine tussock gives way to damp beech forests before heading into the dripping West Coast rain forest, thick with rampant tree ferns. Step onto the open-air viewing carriage for an even more intimate experience; photo opportunities abound.

At the little alpine community of Arthur's Pass you enter the 8km-long Otira Tunnel, burrowing under the high peaks and emerging at the former rail town of Otira. After losing height quickly along the cascading Taramakau River the train cuts to the tranquil shores of Lake Brunner before the final run down the Grey River to Greymouth.

25 On the right track

coast to coast with the TranzAlpine

need to know

The TranzAlpine (⊛www.tranzscenic.co.nz) operates daily from Christchurch to Greymouth and back, taking around 4hr 30min in each direction with an hour spent in Greymouth. One-way trips start at around NZ$90, day-returns from around NZ$150.

25

Ultimate experiences

New

Zealand

miscellany

1 Maori culture

Maori has always been a strongly **verbal culture**, and oratory remains highly revered in formal situations. Anyone standing up to speak at a *hui* (meeting) or *tangi* (funeral) will first claim their right to speak for their people by reciting their *whakapapa* (genealogy). This is often followed by a reverential nod to the *iwi*'s (tribe's) local mountain, river or bay and maybe a short legend from the *iwi*'s past. Each *iwi* has its own set of legends, but some of the most important stories are shared by *iwi* from across the country. Perhaps the most widely accepted is the creation story.

▶▶ Maui fishes up a whoppa

Demigod trickster, **Maui**, went fishing with his brothers in their canoe. With an enchanted barb he soon hooked an enormous fish which stretched to the horizon in every direction. Using his magic powers, Maui got the fish to lie on the surface where it became New Zealand's North Island, known as Te ika a Maui "the fish of Maui". Maui's brothers began to cut up the fish and eat it, in the process shaping mountains and valleys in its surface. The South Island is often called Te waka a Maui, "the canoe of Maui", and Stewart Island is "the anchor", Te punga o te waka a Maui.

 # 2 Reel New Zealand

The most sensational movies to come out of New Zealand are undoubtedly the *Lord of the Rings* trilogy, but a number of other internationally recognized flicks also showcase the country and its talented film makers.

The Piano (1993). Brooding story of a mute Scottish émigré who uses the piano to express herself.

Once Were Warriors (1994). A brutal tale of a South Auckland Maori family in the 1970s.

Whale Rider (2002). Engaging story of a young girl who defies the patriarchal Maori elders with heart warming results.

The World's Fastest Indian (2005). Uplifting biography of back shed motorbike mechanic Bert Munro who lived his high speed dreams.

Sione's Wedding (2006). Entertaining comedy about four Auckland Samoan lads trying to get steady girlfriends.

3 Learning the lingo

English and Maori share joint status as New Zealand's official languages, but on a day-to-day basis all you'll need is English, or its colourful Kiwi variant. However, for the 50,000 native speakers and 100,000 who speak it as a second tongue, Maori is very much a living language. It is often badly pronounced by white New Zealanders, and consequently most visitors. Here are a few **pronunciation pointers** to help you get it right:

- Long compound words can be split into syllables which all end in a vowel. Waikaremoana comes out as Wai-ka-re-mo-ana.
- All syllables are stressed evenly, so it is not **Wai**-ka-re-mo-ana or Wai-ka-re-**mo**-ana but a flat Wai-ka-re-mo-ana.
- Maori words don't take an "s" to form a plural, so you'll find many plural nouns in this book – kiwi, tui, kauri, Maori – in what appears to be a singular form; about the only exception is Kiwis (as people), a Maori word wholly adopted into English.
- Ng is pronounced much as in "sing".
- Wh sounds either like an aspirated "f " as in "off ", or like the "wh" in "why", depending on who is saying what, and in which part of the country.

In Maori, New Zealand is known as Aotearoa – "the land of the long white cloud". For a list of Maori vocabulary, see "Taking the next step" on the back cover.

 # 4 A question of sport

Rugby is more of a religion than a sport in New Zealand. A single All Black defeat elicits much hand wringing and calls for the head of the coach. Fortunately that doesn't happen very often. However, the team habitually underperforms at the quadrennial Rugby World Cup and hasn't won the competition since the inaugural event in 1985, despite always seeming to enter as favourites. In 2011, when the country is hosting the event, the All Blacks hope to live up to expectations.

5 Adventure activities

New Zealand's dramatically varied geography and range of climatic conditions make it an exceptional place to get the adrenaline pumping, with a host of high-octane pursuits scattered throughout both islands.

▶▶ **5 heart-racing activities**

Bungy jumping Best around Queenstown.

Canyoning Walking, swimming and sliding down a canyon with big jumps and longer abseils. Wanaka, Queenstown or Auckland.

Cave rafting Best in Waitomo, where abseiling is an option and glow-worms add atmosphere.

Whitewater rafting Grip with your legs and paddle like hell. Best around Rotorua, Queenstown and the West Coast.

Tandem skydiving Jumps from as high as 4572m (with optional oxygen) anywhere with fabulous scenery.

 # **Dates for the diary**

Waitangi Day, nationwide (Feb 6). National holiday with formal events, such as the ceremonial launching of the world's largest war canoe, at Waitangi.

Coast-to-Coast, Greymouth (early Feb). New Zealand's longest-running and most prestigious multisport event, involving cycling, mountain running and kayaking a total of 243km.

Pasifika Festival, Auckland (mid-March). Day-long celebration of Pacific island culture with music, food and dance.

Wildfoods Festival, Hokitika (mid-March). An opportunity to sample weird and (sometimes) wonderful culinary concoctions such as fried huhu grubs and marinated goat kebabs.

Matariki, nationwide (June). Celebration of the Maori New Year with street performances, star spotting, tree planting and *hangi* (a traditional Maori feast) nights.

Say what?

To fit in with the locals (or at least understand what they're saying) it's useful to familiarize yourself with some **Kiwi slang**:

Bach holiday home

Back-blocks or wop-wops remote areas

Bludger someone who doesn't chip in

Bro short for brother, a matey term of endearment

Chilly bin insulated cool box for carrying picnic supplies

Choice fantastic

Chook chicken

Chuddy chewing gum

Chunder vomit

Cuz or Cuzzy short for cousin and used much as the same as "Bro"

Dag funny or entertaining character

Dairy corner store

Dob in to report someone to someone in authority

Hoon lout, yob or delinquent

Jafa stands for "Just Another Fucking Aucklander" but used as a noun

Jandals flip flops

Sweet, sweet as Fine, cool

OE overseas experience, usually a year spent abroad by Kiwis in their early twenties

Pike out to chicken out or give up

Stoked very pleased

Squiz a look, as in "give us a squiz"

Togs swimming costume

 Kiwis, kiwi and kiwifruit

Kiwis: any New Zealander

kiwi: endangered flightless bird and New Zealand's national symbol

kiwifruit: brown-skinned, green-fleshed fruit. Kiwis never call it a kiwi, always a kiwifruit

A fiery nature

New Zealand sits astride the Pacific and Australian tectonic plates, on the Pacific Ring of Fire. The major faultline runs from the actively volcanic White Island in the north, through steamy Rotorua and Taupo, through shaky Wellington and down the length of the Southern Alps in the South Island.

▶▶ 5 top hot springs to visit

Hot Water Beach Come at low tide, rent a spade and dig yourself a hot pool beside the cool surf.

Polynesian Spa Commercial resort in Rotorua with mineral pools, family spa, adult-only open-air complex and all manner of body treatments.

Kerosene Creek Hot springs well up into a cool stream. Popular day and evening.

Maruia Springs Small resort in the hills 200km north of Christchurch. Particularly magical in winter.

Welcome Flat Hot Springs Four natural pools gloriously situated amid mountain scenery just south of Fox Glacier. It is a 6–7hr walk-in and you can stay at the adjacent Department of Conservation (DOC) hut.

 # Sheep, sheep and more sheep

New Zealand has around 40 million **sheep**, roughly ten for every citizen, down from a twenty to one ratio a couple of decades back. Government subsidies supported an artificially large sheep population and when the subsidies were withdrawn, the sheep numbers dropped. Sales of wool and lamb make up around ten percent of New Zealand's exports, worth around $3 billion a year.

In the first week of March, the town of Masterton holds the **Golden Shears**, essentially the Olympiad of all things woolly. Kiwi shearing superstar David Fagan has won the competition sixteen times as well as being world shearing champion on five occasions. He has been known to shear a lamb in sixteen seconds.

Tongue twisters

A hill in southern Hawke's Bay boasts the world's longest place name, **Taumatawhakatangihangakoauauotamateaturipukakapikimaungahoronukapokaiwhenuakitanatahu**. This roughly translates as "the hill where Tamatea, circumnavigator of the lands, played the flute for his lover".

▸▸ Maori words which combine to form place names

Ara path

Awa river

Iti small

Kino bad

Manga stream

Maunga mountain

Moana sea or lake

Motu island

Nui big

O place of

One sand or beach

Pa fort

Pae ridge

Puke hill

Puna spring

Rangi sky

Roa long or high

Roto lake

Rua hole or pit

Tai sea

Tapu sacred

Tara peak

Te the

Tomo cave

Wai water

Waka canoe

Examples: **Waitomo** (water cave), **Rotorua** (lake hole), **Maunganui** (big mountain), **Awaroa** (long river).

 # Unforgettable routes

▸▸ Five great drives

East Cape, North Island. Slow to the pace of this staunchly Maori rural area.

Ninety Mile Beach, Northland. Brave the quicksands of Te Paki stream and drive this immense beach.

Catlins Coast, Southland. Take it slow, stopping off for penguin-viewing, short walks and the chance to see dolphins cavorting in the surf.

West Coast, South Island. Wild, surf-lashed beaches, luxuriant bush, glaciers and classic Kiwi pubs.

The road to Milford Sound, Fiordland. Fabulous lake views, heaps of walks, hanging glaciers and the country's second longest road tunnel.

Nature calls

New Zealand's native birds evolved without mammalian predators, and most of them subsequently lost the ability to fly. With the arrival of humans, many species died out, and the majority of those that remain – even the kiwi – cling on precariously, often surviving only with human help.

▶▶ Birds on the brink

Black stilt / kaki (pop. 60). A denizen of South Island braided rivers, this population is recovering from a low of just 23 twenty years ago.

Kakapo (pop. 86). Huge green flightless parrot which only exists on intensively managed islands.

Orange-fronted parakeet (pop. 100–200). Forest parakeet vigilantly maintained to save it from rat and stoat predators.

Takahe (pop. 250). Red-beaked, turkey-sized ground-dweller long thought extinct and rediscovered in 1948.

Black Robin (pop. 250). Tiny bird whose numbers were down to 5 (just a single breeding pair) in 1980.

"I was awakened by the singing of the birds ashore…. they seemed to strain their throats with emulation, and made, perhaps, the most melodious wild music I have ever heard, almost imitating small bells, but with the most tunable silver imaginable."

Joseph Banks, 1770

▶▶ Five top bird sanctuaries

Kapiti Island, near Wellington. The country's first wildlife sanctuary, established in 1897. Now largely predator-free.

Karori Sanctuary, Wellington. In the late 1990s this became New Zealand's original urban sanctuary. It pioneered the predator-proof fence which surrounds it and which is increasingly used around similar sanctuaries throughout the country.

Maungatautari, central North Island. Ambitious 3000-hectare inland sanctuary soon to be surrounded by a 47km predator-proof fence.

Tiritiri Matangi Island, near Auckland. Wonderfully accessible open sanctuary full of bird life.

Ulva Island, Stewart Island. Small island sanctuary with some amazingly tame birds, particularly the robins which often peck seeds from around your feet if you stand still.

 # Great escapes

First-rate accommodation options can be found tucked away in some of the country's most idyllic spots, making for some truly effective rest and relaxation.

▶▶ 5 top luxury retreats

Blanket Bay Lodge, Glenorchy. An A-list hangout with fabulous *Lord of the Rings* scenery. Seclusion and discretion guaranteed.

Huka Lodge, Taupo. Consistently rated among the world's finest lodges since 1984, when it was the first of its kind in New Zealand.

Treetops Luxury Lodge and Estate, Rotorua. Low-key luxury in a wonderful forest setting.

Wharekauhau, Featherstone. Elegant, Edwardian-style lodge on a large farm ten minutes by helicopter from Wellington.

Kauri Cliffs Lodge, Kerikeri. Gorgeous sea views and New Zealand's finest golf course.

 # Kiwi tunes

Kiwi bands **Split Enz**, **The Chills**, and **The Datsuns** have had some international recognition over the years. Many bands rarely get heard outside New Zealand, but the local scene is more vibrant than ever.

▶▶ 5 Kiwi bands to check out

The Mint Chicks Grungy, punk fun.

The Black Seeds Dubbed-down Wellington reggae.

Pluto Classic pop rock with great hooks.

Che Fu R&B and hip-hop with a Pacific flavour.

Nesian Mystik Poppy Polynesian hip-hop.

16 A Kiwi flavour

New Zealand doesn't have a cuisine as such. A culinary heritage based on the British and Irish roots of many of the colonists is still evident, but most restaurants now draw on a bewildering array of international influences – often on the same menu. Restaurant locations, especially those waterside, can sometimes be just as spectacular as your meal. Maori food is rarely seen in restaurants but one treat worth seeking out is the traditional Maori **hangi**, a communal affair in which heaps of meat and veg are cooked in an earth oven.

▶▶ 5 tastes not to miss

- **Whitebait**
- **Bluff oysters**
- **Feijoas** (green-skinned fruit a bit like a guava)
- **Marlborough Sauvignon Blanc**
- **Central Otago Pinot Noir**

▶▶ 5 rural waterside restaurants

- **The Waterline**, Kohukohu, Northland
- **The Store**, Kekerengu Point, Marlborough
- **Fleur's Place**, Moeraki, Otago
- **The Bay House**, Tauranga Bay, West Coast
- **Wharfside Café**, Oban, Stewart Island

17 The social laboratory

New Zealand has continually striven to forge a new and better society. In the 1890s it was tagged the "social laboratory of the world".

▶▶ Leading the world

First country to give full **women's suffrage** (1893).

First country to introduce compulsory **industrial arbitration** (1894).

One of the first countries to introduce **old age pension** (1898).

First **welfare state** with free health service, family benefits, state housing and increased pensions (1935).

A multicultural population

New Zealand has a population of 4.1 million people of whom three quarters live in the North Island, 1.25 million of them in the Auckland conurbation. Maori, Pacific Island and Asian populations are all increasing faster than the New Zealand average.

▶▶ Population statistics

	NZ	Auckland
European	70%	64%
Maori	15%	10%
Pacific Island	6%	12%
Asian	8%	13%
Other	1%	1%

▶▶ 5 Famous New Zealanders

Edmund Hillary. The first person to climb Mount Everest in 1953.

Peter Jackson. Star director of the *Lord of the Rings* trilogy and *King Kong* amongst others.

Ernest Rutherford. Nobel Prize winning scientist who first split the atom in 1911.

Jonah Lomu. Big fella. Plays rugby quite well.

Michael Campbell. Winner of the 2005 US golf open and probably the world's most famous Maori.

"We knocked the bastard off."

Sir Edmund Hillary after reaching the summit of Everest

 # An old inhabitant

Little changed in 225 million years, the 30cm-long lizard-like **tuatara** is New Zealand's "living dinosaur". The last of its relatives died out 60 million years ago. The tuatara's forehead contains a third eye which, in the young, is visible under the skin and is sensitive to ultraviolet radiation. This helps produce vitamin D which helps the tuatara grow.

20 Nuclear-free New Zealand

New Zealanders have long prided themselves on their **nuclear-free nation**. In 1973 the government dispatched two frigates to Mururoa to protest against French atmospheric testing in the Pacific. By 1984, New Zealand required foreign vessels entering its ports to be nuclear-free, a move which forced New Zealand out of a defence pact with Australia and the US.

A year later, French government agents blew up the Greenpeace flagship *Rainbow Warrior* as it prepared to protest a new round of French testing at Mururoa. The agents were caught and tried, but France used all its international clout to get them repatriated, and subsequently gave them military honours.

21 Clean, green New Zealand

New Zealand successfully markets itself as being clean and green, but the purity is largely accidental. With a relatively low population density, fresh cleansing Pacific winds and enough rainfall to sluice away the filth, New Zealand gets away with relatively lax pollution controls.

▶▶ Current conservation issues

Rotorua lakes dying from nutrient-rich agricultural runoff.

Invasive alga didymo (aka rock snot) clogging up South Island lakes and rivers.

Possums, **stoats** and **rats** killing threatened native birds.

The search for more **energy**. Whether to dam rivers, buy expensive oil, burn dirty coal or, the big taboo, go nuclear.

Surf and sand

▶▶ Five favourite beaches

Whale Bay, Northland. Small, secluded and occasionally visited by dolphins.

Karekare, Auckland. Classic Kiwi surf beach. Scenes from *The Piano* were shot here.

Cathedral Cove, Coromandel Peninsula. Warm sands, limpid waters and a magnificent rock architecture.

Castlepoint, Wairarapa. Wild and off the beaten track, with lagoon swimming.

Kaiteriteri, near Abel Tasman National Park. Archetypal Kiwi family holiday beach.

 # History

▶▶ A few key dates

1200–1300	Arrival of first **Polynesians**.
1642	Dutchman **Abel Tasman** sails past the West Coast but doesn't land.
1769	Englishman **James Cook** circumnavigates both main islands and makes first constructive contact.
1840	Maori chiefs sign **Treaty of Waitangi**, effectively making New Zealand British.
1860–65	**Land Wars** between Pakeha (white New Zealanders) and Maori.
1947	New Zealand becomes fully independent from Britain
1960s	Start of **immigration from Pacific Islands**. Major **urbanization of Maori** population.
1984	Widespread privatization and deregulation of NZ's protectionist economy.
1997	Jenny Shipley becomes NZ's **first woman Prime Minister**.
2001–03	NZ in the spotlight as the three *Lord of the Rings* movies are released to general acclaim.
2005	**Maori Party** formed. Claims four Maori parliamentary seats.

24 NZ on paper

▶▶ Five top books by New Zealanders

The Bone People Keri Hulme. Mystical, Booker prize winning novel set on the South Island's West Coast.

Collected Stories Katherine Mansfield. Amassed works of one of the world's finest ever short story writers.

The Plumb Trilogy Maurice Gee. Powerful novels covering three generations of Kiwis, by one of New Zealand's most distinguished living writers.

An Angel at My Table Janet Frame. Skilled novelist perhaps best known for this three-volume autobiography.

Stonedogs Craig Marriner. Gangs, drugs and murder: the 2002 breakthrough novel by one of the faces of modern Kiwi writing.

25 Technological pioneers

Kiwi pioneers were forced to make do with what they had and became inveterate tinkerers. The Kiwi bloke's shed became his haven, and a few men came to exemplify the breed.

Richard Pearce Self-taught inventor who, eight months before the Wright Brothers' famous "first flight", flew his flimsy monoplane 140 metres before crashing into a gorse hedge. His inability to land safely invalidated his efforts – not that he bothered to even tell anyone what he'd achieved.

Bill Hamilton Pioneered water-jet powered boats in the 1950s to provide access along narrow braided rivers to his large high-country sheep farm. His boats could skim along in water as little as 100mm deep and turn within their own length, qualities which spawned a lucrative tourism industry.

Burt Munro Little known until the 2005 movie *The World's Fastest Indian*, Bill Munro spent years in his primitive workshop squeezing every bit of power he could from a 1920 Indian motorcycle. Burrowing himself away for 80-hour weeks, he eventually emerged for speed trials, and in 1967 at 306kmph, his Indian became the world's fastest, a record it holds today.

Ultimate experiences New Zealand small print

New Zealand
The complete experience

ROUGH GUIDES – don't just travel

We hope you've been inspired by the experiences in this book. To us, they sum up what makes New Zealand such an extraordinary and stimulating place to travel. There are 24 other books in the 25 Ultimate Experiences series, each conceived to whet your appetite for travel and for everything the world has to offer. As well as covering the globe, the 25s series also includes books on **Journeys, World Food, Adventure Travel, Places to Stay, Ethical Travel, Wildlife Adventures** and **Wonders of the World**.

When you start planning your trip, Rough Guides' new-look guides, maps and phrasebooks are the ultimate companions. For 25 years we've been refining what makes a good guidebook and we now include more colour photos and more information – on average 50% more pages – than any of our competitors. Just look for the sky-blue spines.

Rough Guides don't just travel – we also believe in getting the most out of life without a passport. Since the publication of the bestselling Rough Guides to **The Internet** and **World Music**, we've brought out a wide range of lively and authoritative guides on everything from **Climate Change** to **Hip-Hop**, from **MySpace** to **Film Noir** and from **The Brain** to **The Rolling Stones**.

Publishing information

Rough Guide 25 Ultimate experiences New Zealand Published May 2007 by Rough Guides Ltd, 80 Strand, London WC2R 0RL
345 Hudson St, 4th Floor,
New York, NY 10014, USA
14 Local Shopping Centre, Panchsheel Park,
New Delhi 110017, India
Distributed by the Penguin Group
Penguin Books Ltd,
80 Strand, London WC2R 0RL
Penguin Group (USA)
375 Hudson Street, NY 10014, USA
Penguin Group (Australia)
250 Camberwell Road, Camberwell,
Victoria 3124, Australia
Penguin Books Canada Ltd,
10 Alcorn Avenue, Toronto, Ontario,
Canada M4V 1E4
Penguin Group (NZ)
67 Apollo Drive, Mairangi Bay, Auckland 1310, New Zealand

Printed in China
© Rough Guides 2007
No part of this book may be reproduced in any form without permission from the publisher except for the quotation of brief passages in reviews.
80pp
A catalogue record for this book is available from the British Library
ISBN: 978-1-84353-825-7
The publishers and authors have done their best to ensure the accuracy and currency of all the information in **Rough Guide 25 Ultimate experiences New Zealand**, however, they can accept no responsibility for any loss, injury, or inconvenience sustained by any traveller as a result of information or advice contained in the guide.

1   3   5   7   9   8   6   4   2

Rough Guide credits

Editor: Nikki Birrell
Design: Katie Stephens
Picture editor: Jj Luck
Cartography: Maxine Repath, Katie Lloyd-Jones

Proofreader: Lucy White
Production: Aimee Hampson, Katherine Owers
Cover design: Diana Jarvis, Chloë Roberts

The author

Paul Whitfield writes the Rough Guide to New Zealand.

Picture credits

Fly Less – Stay Longer!

Rough Guides believes in the good that travel does, but we are deeply
aware of the impact of fuel emissions on climate change. We recommend
taking fewer trips and staying for longer. If you can avoid travelling by air,
please use an alternative, especially for journeys of under 1000km/600miles.
And always offset your travel at www.roughguides.com/climatechange.

ROUGH GUIDES

New Zealand

Budapest

Thailand

Greece

Punk

Italy

India

Over 70 reference books and hundreds of travel
guides, maps & phrasebooks that cover the world

ROUGH GUIDES

ROUGH GUIDES

ROUGH GUIDES

ROUGH GUIDES

ROUGH GUIDES

ROUGH GUIDES

ROUGH GUIDES

Australia

Cuba

Britain

Singapore

Vietnam

New York City

Index